942.40

D1340599

COUNTRY
NEWBURY BERKSHIRE

0132244065

First published 1994
This new edition 2008
© Richard Shurey 1994, 2008

COUNTRYSIDE BOOKS
3 Catherine Road
Newbury, Berkshire

To view our complete range of books,
please visit us at
www.countrysidebooks.co.uk

ISBN 978 1 84674 095 4

Cover picture of Ilmington
supplied by Bill Meadows

Maps by the author and
redrawn by CJWT Solutions

Produced through MRM Associates Ltd., Reading
Typeset by CJWT Solutions, St Helens
Printed by Information Press, Oxford

*All material for the manufacture of this book
was sourced from sustainable forests*

Contents

AREA MAP SHOWING LOCATIONS OF THE WALKS

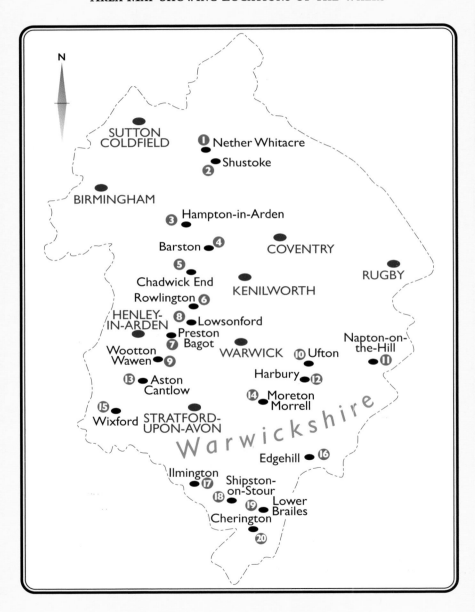

N

SUTTON COLDFIELD

❶ Nether Whitacre

❷ Shustoke

BIRMINGHAM

❸ Hampton-in-Arden

Barston ❹

COVENTRY

❺

Chadwick End

KENILWORTH

RUGBY

Rowlington ❻

HENLEY-IN-ARDEN ❽ Lowsonford

Preston Bagot
❼

Wootton Wawen ❾

WARWICK

❿ Ufton

Napton-on-the-Hill

⓫

Harbury ⓬

⓭ Aston Cantlow

⓮ Moreton Morrell

⓯
Wixford

STRATFORD-UPON-AVON

Warwickshire

Edgehill ⓰

Ilmington ⓱

Shipston-on-Stour

⓲

⓳ Lower Brailes

Cherington

⓴

PUBLISHER'S NOTE

We hope that you obtain considerable enjoyment from this book; great care has been taken in its preparation. However, changes of landlord and actual closures are sadly not uncommon. Likewise, although at the time of publication all routes followed public rights of way or permitted paths, diversion orders can be made and permissions withdrawn.

We cannot, of course, be held responsible for such diversion orders and any inaccuracies in the text which result from these or any other changes to the routes, nor any damage which might result from walkers trespassing on private property. We are anxious though that all details covering the walks and the pubs are kept up to date and would therefore welcome information from readers which would be relevant to future editions.

The simple sketch maps that accompany the walks in this book are based on notes made by the author whilst checking out the routes on the ground. However, for the benefit of a proper map, we do recommend that you purchase the relevant Ordnance Survey sheet covering your walk. The Ordnance Survey maps are widely available, especially through booksellers and local newsagents.

INTRODUCTION

Warwickshire is known as Shakespeare's county. How appropriate, therefore, that he so loved the inns and taverns around Stratford-upon-Avon. I invite you to travel further afield to the far boundaries of the county to seek out walks around some of my favourite pubs in some magnificent countryside. A little apology for the geographical purists – I have taken the Warwickshire borders to be the historic limits before the poaching of land to form the new, unromantic, West Midlands.

There is a wide variety of countryside in Warwickshire. To the north is the area of the old Forest of Arden, where the soils are less fertile and pockets of the ancient woodlands remain to add charm and interest. The south is the Feldon, with clay and good agricultural lands between the Avon and the limestone uplands. This area is more sparsely populated and over half a million acres are still used for farming. The Cotswolds nudge their way into southern Warwickshire to give perhaps the finest rambling terrain, with the hills climbing to 850 ft above sea level. Here there are the villages of honey-hued stone – and delightfully sited pretty pubs which make fine havens after the exertion of climbing the heights.

Although I have tried to describe the routes as accurately as possible, the countryside is constantly changing. Hedgerows can still be removed, trees felled and stiles and footpath signs obliterated. On the plus side, the County Council has been active of late in rescuing pathways and encouraging greater use of the rights of way network. So take care and, if in doubt, ask the locals. In particular Warwickshire County Council has a policy of replacing stiles with kissing gates.

The sketch maps should be sufficient (read with the text of the walk) to follow the routes without difficulty. However, it adds interest to the walk and indicates possible short-cuts if the relevant 1:50 000 Landranger series map is carried.

The car can usually be left in the pub car park whilst doing the walk. However, it is a courtesy to clear this with the landlord.

Children and family parties are now welcomed at most pubs. At many we find such provisions as games rooms, reduced meal portions and garden play areas to burn off surplus energy. However, when there are children in your party please check where children are allowed.

Many of us take our dogs on rambles. I found that my collie cross Meg was invariably welcome; although her manners are impeccable she fully understood when the rule was that dogs remain outside.

Richard Shurey

THE OXFORD CANAL VISITED ON WALK 11

The Dog Inn

THE PLEASANT COUNTRY PATHS ON THIS WALK ARE GENTLY RURAL, ALTHOUGH WITHIN EASY REACH OF BIRMINGHAM. PARTS OF THE ROUTE ARE ALONG THE WAYMARKED PATHS OF THE HEART OF ENGLAND WAY AND THE CENTENARY WAY. THE RETURN LEG BORDERS SHUSTOKE RESERVOIR WHICH (BESIDES PROVIDING SPORT FOR THE ANGLER AND SAILOR) SUPPLIES NUNEATON AND COVENTRY WITH WATER.

The **DOG INN** is along the leafy Dog Lane and a building has been here since the Domesday survey of 1086. It cannot be this place as the Dog is only some 450 years old. It was most probably once a farm, but now a very warm welcome awaits you at this Punch

Taverns house. With masses of brasses and oak wood, it has that comfortable feeling which one expects from a popular country inn. There is an inglenook fireplace and a piano in the lounge. There is also a snug, a dining room and a bar.

In addition to the regular menu, there is a 'specials' board with a frequent change in the bill of fare. The steak chasseur is a favourite dish and the excellent home-made pies are always popular. Meals are served during the summer months in the pretty garden. The real ales offered are Bombardier and guests, and the choice of ciders is between draught Strongbow and Old England. The Dog is open 11 am to 3 pm and 6 pm to 11 pm Monday to Friday and all day Saturday and Sunday. Children can join you at lunchtime, if eating, and Meg was on her best behaviour when I visited and was welcomed.

✆ 01675 481318.

How to get there: Nether Whitacre is on the B4098, about 12 miles east of Birmingham and 3 miles south of Kingsbury. Look for the Dog Inn sign pointing down Dog Lane.

Parking: There is a large car park adjoining the pub.

Length of the walk: 4 miles. Map: OS Landranger series 139 Birmingham and surrounding area (GR 233930).

THE WALK

1 On entering the lane from the car park, turn left. Within a few steps a path is signed down a vehicle way on the right. At the end enter a sometimes arable field. Follow the arrowed direction (or walk around the edge) to a stile leading to the B4098. Turn right. Within ½ mile and opposite a lane, turn left over a stile. In the field, follow the indicated direction to climb a stile in the opposite boundary. Keep on this heading to a stile leading to a lane.

2 Turn right. Just before a railway bridge the path is down a

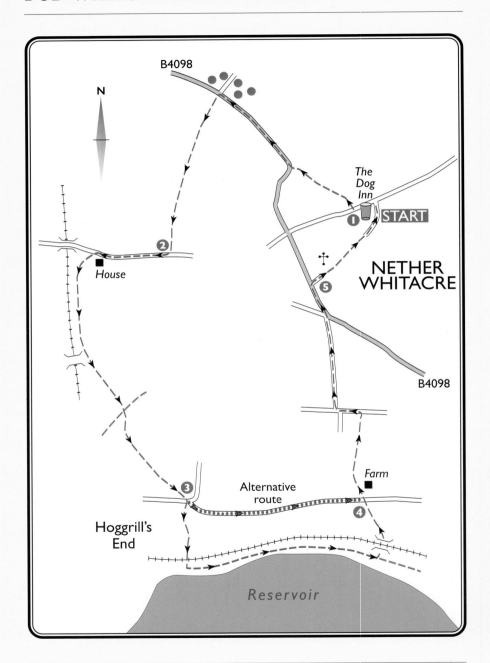

B4098

N

The
Dog
Inn

START

NETHER
WHITACRE

House

B4098

Farm

Alternative
route

Hoggrill's
End

Reservoir

HOGGRILL'S END

vehicle way, left. Past the houses, go left to walk alongside the railway, then, by a footbridge, bear left away from the railway. The path is well marked to a junction of paths. Follow the **Heart of England Way** arrows to cut off the corner of the field. Bear left at the edge of the arable field. Continue ahead to climb a corner stile into another field (still the Heart of England Way). Note – this path may be temporarily closed due to engineering work. If closed take the opposite lane.

3 Go diagonally across to a stile, then on to a lane by a junction. Cross to the signed path opposite, which goes around the edge of gardens to a field. Follow the path to a railway. Just beyond is a junction of paths. Turn left. The track borders the reservoir

(on the right) and the railway (on the left) for about ¾ mile. Look for a path going left under the railway to a field and bear left to climb out of the vale.

4 Aim to the left of a farmhouse and climb a stile to a lane. Almost opposite, a path is signed up the bank. Follow the indicated direction, taking great care over the very rough ground. Within a few yards, climb a stile to an arable field. Walk down the field to the stile, midway in the far boundary. Over the stile, walk by a left-hand hedge to a step stile onto a lane. Turn left, then right at the crossroads. At the B4098 turn left. Keep to the right of an inn.

5 Within 200 yards, turn right down the church drive. Walk through the churchyard, keeping the church on the left. A lane is reached and this leads directly to the **Dog Inn**.

The Plough Inn

THE WALK STARTS ON THE VILLAGE GREEN, WHERE THERE IS AN ANCIENT ANIMAL POUND. THERE IS THEN A LANE WHICH BORDERS SHUSTOKE RESERVOIR (WHICH SUPPLIES COVENTRY) – THE WATERS ARE USED FOR SAILING AND FISHING. WE FOLLOW, FOR A FEW MILES, THE ROUTE OF THE HEART OF ENGLAND WAY, A LONG-DISTANCE FOOTPATH STRETCHING FROM CANNOCK CHASE TO THE COTSWOLDS.

The **PLOUGH INN** has overlooked the little village green for over 200 years. During this time it has not always been an inn, though.

It was once two farm workers' cottages. During the last war, it housed troops for a while. They no doubt also enjoyed the tranquil countryside around Shustoke.

THE PLOUGH is friendly and relaxed; a cosy country pub with a labyrinth of rooms with settles in the corners. All the rooms (interconnected to the one bar) have old prints, faded framed newspapers, cart wheels and other memorabilia – many things to stimulate interesting conversation. That one bar is well known to knowledgeable beer drinkers. It serves Banks's and Black Sheep beers, guest ales and a good selection of lagers.

The menu is ideal for ramblers who have worked up an appetite, and the 'toasties', home-cooked ham and home-baked pies are very popular. The lunchtime opening hours are 12 noon to 3 pm (Monday to Friday) and all day Saturday and Sunday. Evening hours are variable. Food is available every day. Children have their own menu, with their favourite beans on toast and chips. Outside, there is a small garden. My Meg was welcomed and could join the three dogs who are 'regulars'.

✆ 01675 481557.

How to get there: The pub is in the centre of Shustoke on the B4114, just 2 miles east of Coleshill.
Parking: There is a small car park by the pub.
Length of the walk: 5 miles. Map: OS Landranger series 139 Birmingham and surrounding area (GR 227909).

THE WALK

1. From the pub cross the road to walk along **Bixhill Lane**. This becomes a footpath and follows first the edge of fields, then left-hand woods. At the end of the woodlands is a stile and a signed meeting of paths. Do not climb the stile but retrace a few steps, then cut across the open field, passing an isolated oak to a stile in the far corner (now following the Heart of England Way

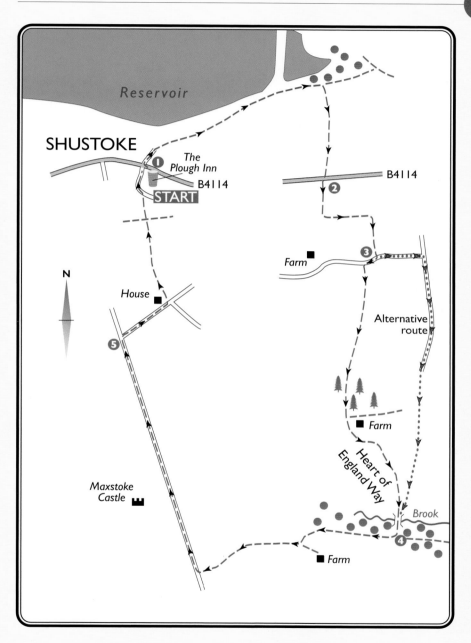

SHUSTOKE

Reservoir

The Plough Inn

START

B4114

B4114

N

House

Farm

Alternative route

5

Heart of England Way

Maxstoke Castle

Farm

Brook

Farm

SHUSTOKE RESERVOIR

waymarks). Walk at the right-hand border of the next field to the main road.

2 Cross to the stile opposite. Follow the waymarking arrows around fields to a lane.

3 Turn right. As the lane twists right, keep ahead along a signed path. Climb a stile, then maintain the direction over the open field. Keep ahead with stiles to show the way to pass to the right of a wood to a vehicle track by a cottage. The path crosses the drive then bears left over the field. At a marker post turn right. Follow the edge of the field to a gap in the hedge, then take the direction of the waymark arrow to pass to the right of an isolated tree to a wood. Go over a brook and keep ahead through trees to a stile. Turn right to walk by a right-hand wood.

(4) At the corner of the woods, climb a stile and bear left in the pasture (with the delightfully-named **Dumble Farm** on the left) to a stile onto the drive. Turn right to a lane and turn right again. We pass the entrance to **Maxstoke Castle**. This 14th-century castle (not open to the public) has often been used in films.

(5) At a junction, turn right along **Hollyland**. By the next junction (at the far side of a yellow house on the left), take a signed path. In the field follow the indicated direction, aiming to the left of a distant house. Using stiles, cross a vehicle way. Walk by a right-hand hedge to a corner stile. Continue beside gardens and cut over the grass to a road. Turn left. This road leads back to the **Plough Inn**.

The White Lion

'AY NOW I AM IN ARDEN THE MORE FOOL I,' SAID TOUCHSTONE IN *AS YOU LIKE IT*. NOT TRUE, FOR IN THE OLD FOREST OF ARDEN IS SOME GENTLE, DELIGHTFUL COUNTRYSIDE. EARLY ON THE WALK THE ROUTE CROSSES THE LITTLE RIVER BLYTHE, OVER A 500-YEAR-OLD PACKHORSE BRIDGE. ACROSS THE MAIN ROAD IS QUIET COUNTRYSIDE BEFORE THE HALFWAY VILLAGE OF BERKSWELL. HERE THERE IS A WEALTH OF FASCINATING THINGS, INCLUDING THE ANCIENT WELL WHERE MONKS WERE BAPTISED, THE STOCKS (WITH FIVE HOLES TO ACCOMMODATE A ONE-LEGGED OFFENDER WITH HIS COMPANIONS), A LITTLE MUSEUM, AND THE INTERESTING CHURCH. THE RETURN SECTION GOES ALONGSIDE A WOOD WHICH IS SCENTED BY BLUEBELLS IN SPRINGTIME.

◆●●◆

The **WHITE LION** is a welcoming hostelry. There was an inn mentioned in Domesday (1086) as being opposite the church in

Hampton. Whether this was on exactly the same site as the White Lion, the licensee of this Punch Taverns house could not say. Records do verify, however, that good ale and food has been offered here for 400 years.

The two front bars are the Lion's Den and Daniel's Bar. The latter I found a gem of a place – a dozen drinkers and it is packed. Dog Meg was allowed to join me, though. A fixed wooden settle and a bench have perhaps not been in place for all the 400 years, but certainly a great many of them. There is more comfort in the larger bar and at the rear is a modern restaurant. The meals are all home-made and very appetising. The steaks are renowned but I like the sound of the Spicy Barbecue Platter, made up of minted lamb chop, spare rib and chicken. Children can have half portions and there is also a children's menu. Vegetarians too, are well catered for. The selection of beers is Brew XI, Old Hookie, Adnams, Black Sheep and a guest. There is a small grassed area with benches and tables and the front of the building also serves as the village notice board, with a host of activities advertised. The hours of opening are 12 noon to 11 pm (every day).
☎ 01675 442833.

How to get there: Hampton-in-Arden is midway between Solihull and Meriden on the B4102. The White Lion is on the edge of the village, opposite the church.
Parking: The car park is off the B4102 at the rear of the pub.
Length of the walk: 6 miles. Map: OS Landranger series 139 Birmingham and surrounding area (GR 204808).

THE WALK

1 From the car park, turn left on the B4102. Almost at once, turn left again down **Marsh Lane**. Within ¼ mile and opposite **Elm Tree Close**, go over a stile by a gate on the right. Walk down the elongated pasture to a stile in the far left corner. At once, climb another stile to a cul-de-sac road. Turn left for a few steps. As

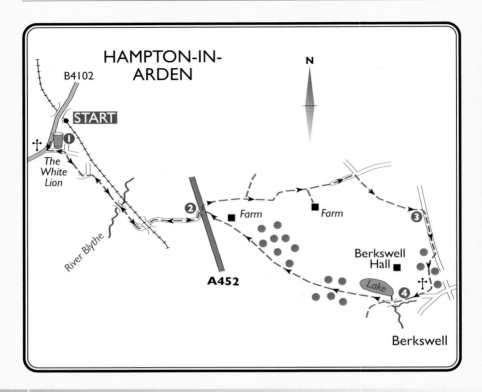

the road twists sharp left, the path is signed ahead along a house drive. Keep ahead to climb a stile, then walk alongside a fence to a stile into a pasture. Maintain the direction to a stile by a gate into an often sown field. The heading is arrowed to follow a route gradually nearing the railway embankment on the left. Follow the way, going over the packhorse bridge, then joining a vehicle way and lane. Follow the lane left under the railway and continue along it to the main A452 road.

2 Almost opposite, a bridleway is signed along a 'private' farm road. Keep on the farm road, passing the farm drive, and continue to a junction. The next path is signed through a gate on the right. Take the direction indicated to cross the field to a stile in the opposite hedge. Maintain the heading over a pasture to drop down to the far left corner. Climb a stile by a gate (dog flap for your Fido and my Meg), but watch the mud.

Continue for a few yards alongside a right-hand wire fence, then maintain the direction to the next stile in a hedge. Beyond, walk near a right-hand hedge to a fence stile by a gate to the left of a white cottage. Turn right on the road.

3 Just before houses on the left, pass through a kissing-gate on the right. Walk a few steps through the trees to a pasture. Walk by the left-hand border, with the elegant 18th-century **Berkswell Hall** away to the right. Go along the edge of the churchyard to a road at **Berkswell**. Turn right through the church gate and continue alongside a wall, keeping the church on your right.

4 Maintain the direction, passing through two kissing-gates into a pasture and along a wooden causeway above a stream. Go over a bridge and walk through a wood. There is a kissing-gate onto a cart track. Cross straight over, along a path signed to **Hampton**. The path is well trodden over an open field to a distant stile. Beyond, walk at the borders of woods and fields. Go over a stile to pastureland and keep the heading to a farmstead. On the drive, turn left to the main road. Cross to rejoin the outward route and retrace your steps to **Hampton** and the **White Lion**.

4 BARSTON

The Bull's Head

THE FIRST MILE OR SO IS OVER FARMLAND (CROSSING THE LITTLE RIVER BLYTHE) ON THE WAY TO TEMPLE BALSALL. THE LAND HERE WAS GIVEN TO THE KNIGHTS TEMPLAR (WHO PROTECTED PILGRIMS TO THE HOLY LAND) IN 1150. THERE IS A HISTORIC CHURCH AND ELEGANT ALMSHOUSES, DATED LATE 17TH CENTURY, CLUSTERED AROUND A BROAD COURTYARD AND AN ANCIENT REFECTORY. ON THE RETURN THE 19TH-CENTURY SPRINGFIELD HOUSE (NOW A SCHOOL) IS PASSED.

The **BULL'S HEAD** is a listed building with a history going back to 1490. There is even a priest hiding-hole upstairs. The quiet lane outside was once the main coaching route between Coventry and Birmingham and the inn, at that time, provided overnight accommodation and had many stables at the rear.

This is a typical village pub. If you want loud pop music and fruit machines this is not the place for you. But if you want cosy bars and good food and ale, mine hosts Martin and Joy Bradley will give you a warm welcome.

There are two bars, but of especial interest to the many parties of walkers is the small dining place at the rear, where the old timbers in the walls and ceilings make this a unique room full of atmosphere of days long past. There is a wide variety of wall furnishings that will stimulate conversation, including several old newspapers which have been framed. I enquired about the availability of one of the products advertised in 1930 – Kruschen Salts (price 6d) which are guaranteed to remove the aches of rheumatism within two weeks! Alternatively, there is an AJS motor cycle for £39.

The food is traditional pub fare, much of it home-cooked, with a particularly interesting range of sandwiches. The opening hours are 11 am to 2.30 pm and 5 pm to late and all day Saturday and Sunday. The real ales served are well-kept Adnams, Old Hookie and a guest. The resident dogs welcome the companions of regular customers so probably Fido will find a friend (but not in the food areas, of course). For warmer days, there are plenty of tables and benches in the gardens to the rear and side of the pub.

✆ 01675 442830.

How to get there: Barston lies south-east of Solihull. Approaching from the B4102 Henley-in-Arden road, turn just by a canal bridge, 1 mile from Solihull. Barston is reached after 3 miles. The Bull's Head is on the left at the start of the village.

Parking: There is a car park at the rear.

Length of the walk: 4 miles. Map: OS Landranger series 139 Birmingham and surrounding area (GR 207781).

THE WALK

1 On the lane from the car park turn left, then almost at once right, through the main church gates (with a lantern above) to

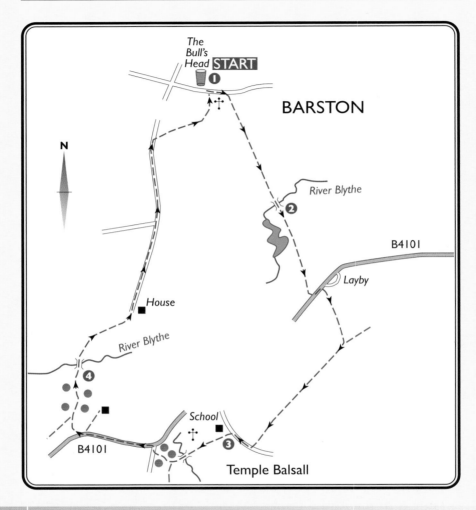

The Bull's Head START ❶

BARSTON

N

River Blythe

❷

B4101

Layby

House

River Blythe

❹

School

❸

B4101

Temple Balsall

the churchyard of **Barston's St Swithin's church,** built of small bricks in 1721. Keeping to the left of the building, continue to the stile into a pasture. Follow the clear path to another stile onto often arable lands. Keep ahead, walking with a hedge on the right-hand side. In a far corner go through a hedge gap and, keeping in the same direction, walk over the open field to a bridge over the **river Blythe.**

2 We are now in a large arable field. Keep by the right-hand border for about 300 yards, then strke out over the open field. There are few landmarks but, if the route is not worn by feet, aim to the left of distant electricity pylons. Climb a stile onto the B4104 and turn left for 100 yards. Just before a layby, turn right over a rather hidden stile. Follow the left-hand edge of the field. In a far corner go under a fence bar to a junction of paths. Turn right, with a hedge on the right, to a road. Turn right.

3 Just before a school, turn left along a path signed to the church, to pass the almshouses. Follow the path over a brook to the gates of a cemetery. Turn right through a kissing-gate. The path through the woods divides. Take the left-hand fork to a lane. Turn right, then at once left along the B4101. Immediately past the drive to **Springfield House**, take a path on the right (the sign may be broken or missing). Through the trees a drive is reached. Turn right. Just before buildings, turn left along a hedged way to a vehicle way. Follow this for a few yards, with school buildings nearby, then bear left along a track through trees and bushes.

4 Emerging on a meadow through a kissing-gate, continue through gates to cross the once elegant bridge over the river. Join a tractor way which veers right. Go over a stile beside a gate and continue along the way of tractors to a stile onto a lane. Note the nearby house built 'Circa Queen Anne 1664–1714'. Walk along the lane and keep ahead at a junction. Within another ⅓ mile, take a signed path over a stile to the right. Walk up the pasture to the fence stile between two trees. Continue in the next pasture near the left-hand border to a hidden stile in the far left-hand corner. This leads to the churchyard at **Barston** again, then the lane. The **Bull's Head** is to the left.

The Orange Tree

THE WALK STARTS WITH A MILE OR SO ALONG LOVELY WINDING LANES, THEN THERE IS A VIEW OF CHADWICK MANOR WHICH WAS BUILT FOR A MANUFACTURER OF SOAP IN 1875. THE TOWPATH OF THE GRAND UNION CANAL IS USED ON THE RETURN LEG.

❖❖❖

The **ORANGE TREE** combines the cosiness of the country hostelry of the past (the building is 17th-century) with the undoubted value for money and elegance of a modernised pub. There are plenty of corners in the bars for quiet conversation and if the talk drags there are many interesting items decorating the walls.

CHADWICK END – *The Orange Tree*

The range of food is rather up-market, with the duck in an orange sauce being very popular. Vegetarian meals are always available and specials of the day are listed on the colourful blackboard behind the bar. Children are catered for with their own small portions. There is a very attractive garden that resembles a small park, but no dogs at this pub, I'm afraid. The beers on offer are Tetley's, Old Hookie and IPA, and for cider drinkers the choice is between Bulmers and Magners. The pub is open all day (no food Sunday evenings).

✆ 01564 785364.

> **How to get there:** Chadwick End is midway between Warwick and Solihull on the A4141. The Orange Tree is in the middle of the hamlet.
> **Parking:** There is a car park at the front of the pub.
> **Length of the walk:** 5 miles. Map: OS Landranger series 139 Birmingham and surrounding area (GR 207731).

THE WALK

1. From the car park, take care while crossing the busy road. Between the post box and phone box, follow the line of stepping stones in the grass – this marks the way to a footpath. Walk at the rear of the gardens of bungalows. The going may be a little overgrown for a yard or two but the track ends at a stile to an arable field. Walk alongside the left-hand hedge to a far metal gate on to a lane. Turn right, then at once left along **Chadwick Lane**. This is a fine narrow highway.

2. Keep ahead at a junction. Within 400 yards (and by another road junction at **Park Corner**), turn left. The path is signed down a house drive. Keep to the right of the **White House** on the well used track. Pass through a gate to a farm track and go right to pass over a brook,

   The main track bends right to barns but we maintain the old

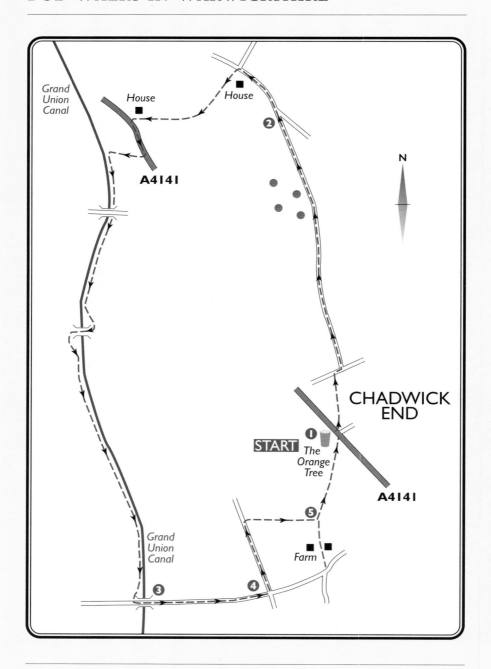

Grand
Union
Canal

House

House

A4141

N

CHADWICK
END

START

The
Orange
Tree

A4141

Grand
Union
Canal

Farm

direction, walking towards a fine house. The path is signed to keep to the left of the garden and house. Pass through a little gate to the main road and turn left for 300 yards. Take a vehicle way, on the right, which leads to an inn and the **Grand Union Canal**. Turn left along the towing path with the water on your right. Stay by the waterway for about 2 miles, with the towing path crossing to the other bank at a bridge.

3 At a road bridge, numbererd '66', leave the canal. Gain the road and turn right to cross the water. At the road junction (with the drive to **Baddesley Clinton Hall** to the right) you have a choice of two routes.

One possibility is to walk straight on at the junction, and take a path signed left down the drive of **Convent Farm**. This avoids a short section on the main route which may be a little muddy and difficult.

4 **For the main walk,** turn left at the road junction and continue for a little under ½ mile. Turn right through an old kissing-gate beside a rough metal gate and follow the farm cart track. When this turns left into a field, maintain the old direction, ignoring the rather confusing waymark arrow. Passing a barrier, follow the clear path through bushes and trees. Pick up the edge of a left-hand pool and continue through the short, possibly boggy, section. Climb a rough fence stile and walk along a wide green way with a hedge to the left and a row of trees to the right. In a corner climb a fence stile and go over a plank bridge. Turn left (barns to the right) to pass through a rough metal gate. The diversion joins the main route here.

5 Walk by a right-hand wide ditch to go through a gate into a ridged pasture. Proceed alongside a right-hand border to climb a rough corner stile. Follow the arrowed directions to continue to a step stile to the main road. The **Orange Tree** is a few steps to the left.

The Tom o' the Wood

The walk starts along the Grand Union Canal, which was formed by amalgamating a number of waterways to link the Midlands with London. A magnificent moated manor house is visited. Baddesley Clinton dates from medieval times and is now in the care of the National Trust.

❖❖❖

The 17th-century **TOM O' THE WOOD** canalside pub shows a windmill on its sign. The licensee told me about the story behind the name. Apparently, Tom owned the sawmill in the hamlet at nearby Finwood. He was a local character and the windmill was called after him. This gave the name to the pub, which had previously been the Old New Inn.

The Tom o' the Wood has a wide range of appetising meals on the menu, and there is an especial 'ploughman's' here. Children are well catered for, with favourites being the pizzas and beefburgers and chips. The real ales offered are Greene King IPA and Spitfire. Ciders include Scrumpy Jack and Strongbow. There are plenty of benches and tables in the pretty gardens, to be enjoyed when the weather permits. My Meg (and other dogs) are asked to remain outside. The pub is open each day from 11 am (Sunday 12 noon).

☎ 01564 782252.

How to get there: Rowington itself lies on the B4439. Approaching from Hockley Heath, go over two canal bridges. One mile further, turn right at a crossroads. The pub is on the left, ½ mile along the lane.

Parking: There is a car park alongside the Tom o' the Wood.

Length of the walk: 4 miles. Map: OS Landranger series 139 Birmingham and surrounding area (GR 195697).

THE WALK

1 From the car park, walk a few steps to the canal. Cross over and at once drop down left to the towing path. Turn left to pass under the lane, with the canal now on your right side. At the next road bridge, go up steps to gain the road.

2 Turn right to walk along the B4439, passing another inn. Within about 200 yards, turn left down a vehicle track (signed as a footpath). Go over a stile by a gate and pass to the right of a large brick building. Go through a gate and take the arrowed direction, passing under high electricity lines.

Continue to the far corner and climb a stile. Maintain the heading, picking up the side of the grounds of **Baddesley Clinton**. This lovely 15th-century house has changed little since 1634. Here you can see priests' secret hiding places, family

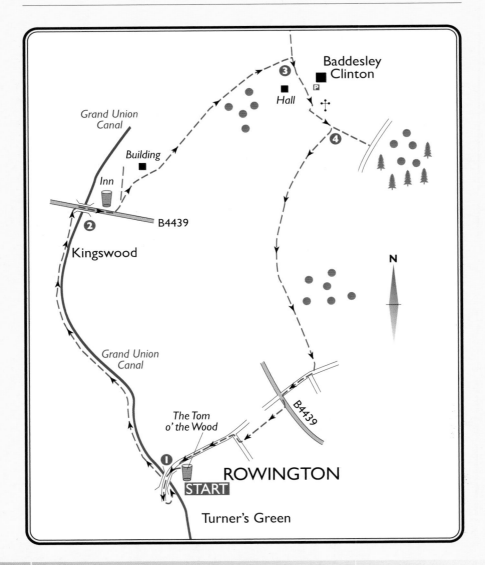

portraits, the old chapel and lovely gardens. Open March to October, afternoons only, Wednesday to Sunday inclusive and on bank holiday Monday afternoons. Continue to the vehicle drive.

THE GRAND UNION CANAL

(3) Turn right. Follow the route for cars but do not turn into the car parking area. Continue, instead, to the entrance of the house. Turn left along a footpath, signed to the church. We are now on the long-distance footpath of the **Heart of England Way**.

Walk along the tree-lined path to **Baddesley Clinton church**. The tower of the lovely building was constructed about 1500 by Nicholas Brome in remorse for having killed a priest. Follow the path through the churchyard to the drive.

(4) Turn right to walk along a fenced track at the side of sheep pastures. Keep on the waymarked path to a lane. Turn right, then left at the B4439. Within a few steps, take a signed path on the right which leads to a lane. Continue right, to a T-junction. Turn left. The **Tom o' the Wood** is ¼ mile along the lane.

The Crab Mill

T HERE ARE SOME MAGNIFICENT PATHWAYS IN THIS PASTORAL COUNTRYSIDE. THE WALK GOES TO YARNINGALE COMMON – ONE OF THE FEW COMMONS REMAINING IN WARWICKSHIRE – AND CROSSES THE STRATFORD CANAL, WHICH WAS COMPLETED IN 1816 TO CONVEY COAL SOUTHWARDS AND CORN AND LIME IN THE OPPOSITE DIRECTION. THE WATERWAY WAS RESTORED BY THE NATIONAL TRUST IN RECENT YEARS.

●◦●

The name of the **CRAB MILL** pub does not refer to seaside crabs but to the wild apples which once grew so profusely in the countryside. Sadly, crab apple trees seem to be a lot rarer these days, with so many hedgerows being grubbed out. We can see on the rather fine sign how the fruit was crushed to make cider and preserves in past days. The building was once an inn for agricultural workers and there are some fascinating prints on the walls of the stone-flagged bar of former rural scenes, such as the steam-powered threshing machine and the women on their knees picking the potato crop.

The Crab Mill is one of the pubs that, in these more enlightened days, stays open all day. It is a freehouse providing meals from 12 noon to 2.30 pm and 6.30 pm to 9.30 pm (Monday to Saturday) and on Sunday, from 12 noon to 3.30 pm only. There is a wide selection of real ales, including Tetleys and Abbott and Purity. Draught Strongbow cider is also available. The menu is extensive, with vegetarians especially well catered for. 'Specials' of the day are chalked on a board behind the bar. This is a family pub and I especially like the welcome to youngsters. They have their own menu (chips with everything, of course).

There is a play area outside the Crab Mill. I think it best if Fido is kept outside.

✆ 01926 843342.

How to get there: The Crab Mill is 1½ miles from Henley-in-Arden, on the A4189 Warwick road.
Parking: There is a car park in front and to the rear of the pub.
Length of the walk: 3 miles. Map: OS Landranger series 151 Stratford-upon-Avon and surrounding area (GR 172653).

THE WALK

1 Turn left out of the car park to walk along the A4189. Within a few steps, take the lane on the left. Keep ahead at a junction. Almost opposite a farm, take a footpath on the right. Climb the hill (passing a seat) to the Norman church of

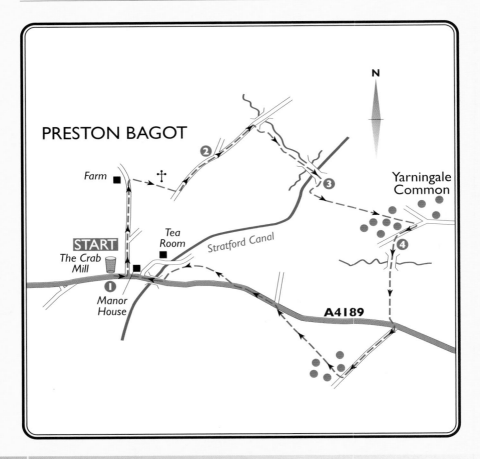

All Saints, Preston Bagot. The trim building has a shingled bell turret. Continue, with the church on the left, to a lane. Turn left.

2 Take the right-hand fork at a Y-junction and drop down the hill. Immediately before a brook, take an unsigned path over a stile on the right. In the pasture, keep near the left-hand brook to meet the canal. Cross the water over the bridge – note the slit down the middle of the bridge which meant the canal bargees did not have to unhitch their horses.

PRESTON BAGOT CHURCH

In the opposite field, bear right to the far left corner. Turn left to walk beside a left-hand hedge. Continue on the same heading, to join a vehicle way to a lane at **Yarningale Common**. Turn right. Within ¼ mile, a path is signed on the left. Walk a few yards through the trees to a step-stile.

3 Continue along a fenced way to climb another stile. Maintain the heading over a brook and continue to the A4189. Cross to the opposite lane. A signed path is indicated on the right after ½ mile. The way is a little muddy to a stile into a field where

BRIDGE OVER THE STRATFORD CANAL

there are game birds' pens. Climb the stile on the top of the rise. Follow the arrowed way to the A4189 again. Turn left. After 300 yards, take the obsolete road on the right. Follow the lane to the A4189. Turn right to the **Crab Mill**, passing (on the right) the 16th-century timbered manor house.

The Fleur de Lys

THE FIRST FOOTPATHS ARE ALONG THE LONG-DISTANCE PATH, THE HEART OF ENGLAND WAY. THE ROUTE IS THROUGH A LANDSCAPE OF GENTLE WOODS AND FIELDS WHICH WERE ONCE PART OF THE VAST FOREST OF ARDEN. THE RETURN TO THE PUB IS ALONGSIDE THE STRATFORD CANAL, WHICH WAS CONSTRUCTED IN 1816. SOME SECTIONS OF THIS WALK CAN BE QUITE MUDDY AT TIMES SO WEAR WELLIES OR STRONG BOOTS.

❖

The 17th-century **FLEUR DE LYS**, which was originally a row of cottages, is full of atmosphere, having ceilings thick with low beams, and up and down stone and tile floors, worn by the feet of countless customers over the centuries. There are many heavy timber roof supports, which means there are hidden alcoves for that cosy tête à tête. The oak furniture enhances the friendly feel and there are three open fires in wintertime.

For the last few decades, the inn has been synonymous with pies. In the 1950s Mr Brookes who was then the landlord started making and selling hot chicken and mushroom pies with peas. In those far off days meals in pubs were rarities – one was lucky to get a rather ancient sandwich or a packet of plain crisps – and the fame of the lovely pies spread far and wide. Today pies (in at least eight varieties) are still made in this delightful old canalside pub but, in addition, many other delectable dishes are available. The frequently changed bill of fare is decoratively chalked on a huge board and some vegetarian meals are always included. The pub is run by Pete Graham and Matt, his son, who ensure the smooth running. The large range of real ales makes a choice difficult. You can choose from Greene King IPA, Abbott and guest beers. For cider lovers there is draught Strongbow and Magners.

There are magnificent lawns, where willows dip low into the canal, and plenty of benches and tables which Fido is allowed to guard. Dogs are permitted in a designated area inside the pub. Children have their play area, with magnificent contraptions on which to climb. There is also a galleried room which is said to be haunted. Youngsters will soon find the toy cupboard after they have selected from their own menu – chips with everything, of course, but healthy fresh vegetables as well. The pub is open all day, every day.

✆ 01564 782431.

How to get there: Lowsonford is signposted from the B4439 Warwick road, about 2 miles from Hockley Heath.
Parking: There is a large car park to the rear of the pub.
Length of the walk: 4 miles. Map: OS Landranger series 151 Stratford-upon-Avon and surrounding area (GR 188678).

THE WALK

1 Out of the car park, turn right along the lane. At a road junction in the centre of the village, turn left by a phone box and walk along a vehicle track. By the cottage at the far end, climb a stile into a pasture. Follow the direction indicated to climb another stile. The path beyond is clear to a cart track. Turn right to cross what was once a bridge over a railway.

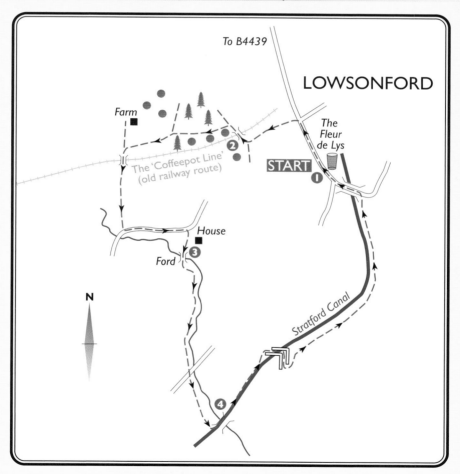

To B4439

LOWSONFORD

Farm

The Fleur de Lys

The 'Coffeepot Line' (old railway route)

2

START **1**

House

Ford **3**

N

Stratford Canal

4

2 Continue to a signed junction of paths. Climb a stile, then at once another, to go 90° left. Walk at the side of an arable field alongside a left-hand wood. Go over a corner stile to enter woods. Follow the clear track through the trees to a pasture. Follow the arrowed way right, to a farm tractor way. Turn left through a metal gate. The tractor way then bends right. Follow this to a stile onto a farm 'road'. Turn left to again cross the old rail route (affectionately known as the 'Coffeepot Line'). Follow the road to a lane. Turn left. Within ⅓ mile, the lane twists sharp left. Go right, down a vehicle way, passing a barn conversion.

3 We come to a ford. There is a footbridge for walkers, but it is not quite long enough, so you may have to use stepping stones to reach the start. Safely over the water, continue along the vehicle way for a further 20 yards. Turn left to take a signed path over a stile.

The path now hugs a left-hand brook through pastures. Keep the water on your left to a stile onto a lane. Cross and climb the stile opposite. Again, keep by the left-hand brook through meadows, to pass through a far white metal gate. The track beyond is often muddy as it nears the canal.

4 Turn left along the towing path. Pass a cottage and an aqueduct where the waterway passes over a stream. At a lock, the towing path crosses to the opposite bank. Note the slit down the bridge which obviated the need for the towing ropes to be unhitched when horses pulled the barges.

Stay on the towing path, passing a nature reserve, to a road bridge (numbered '41'). Just before, go through the gate on the right, onto a lane. Turn left to go over the canal. At a junction, bear right. The **Fleur de Lys** is along the lane on the right.

The Bull's Head

T HE WALK MAINLY FOLLOWS THE BANKS OF TWO WATERWAYS. THE START IS BESIDE THE MEANDERING RIVER ALNE (WHERE YOU MAY BE LUCKY TO SPOT THE ELUSIVE KINGFISHER) AND THE RETURN LEG IS ALONG THE TOWING PATH OF THE STRATFORD CANAL, COMPLETED IN 1816 TO CARRY COAL SOUTHWARDS AND LIMESTONE AND GRAIN IN THE OPPOSITE DIRECTION.

The beautiful old **BULL'S HEAD** carries a date, 1387, so it must be one of the oldest pubs in Warwickshire. It is full of character (some say it is haunted), with thick beams supported on uprights 2 ft thick and stone-flagged floors, worn by countless feet over the centuries. There are blazing log fires to welcome visitors in the winter and the dining room provides old world elegance and is richly furnished.

This is the plaice (sorry!) for lovers of fish dishes. There is every fish dish conceivable chalked on the blackboard, including such delicacies as oysters, lobsters, mussels, crab and squid, besides the usual varieties. To complement the food (which includes plenty of choice for the non-fish eater as well) we find a separate board listing the wines offered and there is a wide selection of real ales, such as Banks' beer and several guests. Children have a separate menu. Dogs must remain outside, I'm afraid. The pub is open from 12 noon to 3 pm Monday to Friday at lunchtimes. Evening hours are from 6 pm to 11 pm. The place is open all day Saturday and Sunday.

⌀ 01564 792511.

How to get there: The pub is on the A3400 between Birmingham and Stratford-upon-Avon, at the junction with the B4089, in the centre of Wootton Wawen.
Parking: There is a car park at the side of the pub.
Length of the walk: 5 miles. Map: OS Landranger series 151 Stratford-upon-Avon and surrounding area (GR 152632).

THE WALK

1 From the car park, cross the B4089 to the cul-de-sac estate road called **The Dale**. At the end of the tarmac road go right, then at once left to walk beside a left-hand wall (with a terrace of houses on the right). Climb a step stile into a pasture. Take the direction arrowed to walk beside hedges to the **river Alne**. Turn right to climb a step stile between the river and a wire fence. Walk beside the right-hand fence (which surrounds a waterworks). Follow the fence to a stile into a pasture. Make for the far right corner to join a vehicle drive then over stiles to a lane.

2 Turn left to cross the river and immediately turn right to go under the railway to a gate into a pasture. Follow the signed

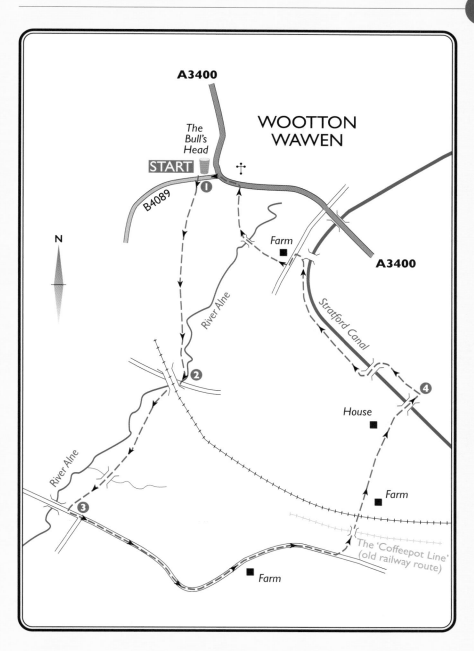

WOOTTON HALL

heading and pass through a gateway (no gate). Bear left. The path is now never far from the right-hand river which we 'nudge' near a farmstead on the opposite bank. In trees, climb a fence stile and continue to a pasture. Bearing slightly left away from the river, make for a railed footbridge now seen. Over a brook, walk the length of a meadow, aiming to the far right corner. Go through a gate to a farm cart track.

3 Follow this to a lane and turn left. Keep on the lane for a little over a mile, then turn left at a signed path to climb a step stile into a field. Cross to the opposite stile. We now cross the long-discarded rail route. This was affectionately known as the 'Coffeepot Line' because (so I am told) of the shape of the locomotive funnel.

Follow the arrowed path over a working railway and climb the gentle hill on the far side, walking alongside the remnants of a right-hand hedge. Climb a stile by a metal gate to join a hedged cart track, then continue ahead. There is a right-hand hedge for 150 yards. Climb a stile, then regain the old heading (left-hand hedge now) to a stile onto a vehicle drive. Turn right.

4 Over the canal bridge, gain the towing path to the left and walk along it, with the water on the left. At the next bridge go over the water. Note the split bridge so the towing ropes of the barges did not have to be unhitched. Continue, with the water now on your right side.

Leave the waterway at the following bridge. Turn left along a vehicle drive (with bungalows on the right) to a lane. Turn left for 100 yards. Go over a stile on the right. In the pasture, walk by a right-hand fence. Waymarks show the route to the bridge to cross the **river Alne.** Turn right along a footpath which runs along the top of an old earthwork. Ahead is the tower of **Wootton Wawen's church.** Keep ahead to the A3400. Turn left and the **Bull's Head** is reached within about 200 yards.

THE STRATFORD CANAL

The White Hart

THE WALK FOLLOWS THE CENTENARY WAY (WARWICKSHIRE'S LONG-DISTANCE PATH, COMPLETED TO MARK THE 100 YEARS OF COUNTY ADMINISTRATION) THROUGH MEADOWLAND, WITH WIDE VISTAS WESTWARDS. ON THE RETURN LEG THERE IS A NATURE RESERVE (ADMINISTERED BY THE WARWICKSHIRE NATURE CONSERVATION TRUST) THROUGH WOODS AND OLD GRAVEL QUARRIES.

❖

The 400-year-old **WHITE HART** is a fun pub where a visit is an occasion, from the friendly welcome from the staff on arrival, to the final drink. The building was originally a workhouse, accommodating the stonemasons constructing St Michael's church across the lane. Now the bars are stone and oak, with the walls decorated with agricultural implements of days past, and there is a homely, relaxing feeling. But you may be tempted to sit in the garden (where there are plenty of tables and benches), for the view over the chequered countryside of the vale of the river Avon is magnificent. The pub is full of interest. You will find traditional darts, football, and dominoes, and stories abound of the pub ghost (a lady). You may also be told of the headless horseman and the phantom coach and horses riding up the hill from the valley.

The range of food and drink in this J.J. Rogers Tavern is extensive, but it is the 'specials' blackboards (which fill a wall) which take the eye. The choice can be from over 50 main dishes (including over a dozen vegetarian). Many are unusual – how about Hart Porky Rack, barbecue ribs of pork with potato fries, followed by Black Bottom Pie, full of cream and chocolate. Curries are a speciality. Eat after the walk and forget the calorie count for the day. There are many real ales from which to select, including Pilgrim and Hook Norton and two guests. There are numerous different coffees too (including the interesting-sounding Parisienne, Monks and Jamaican).

The times of opening are 11.30 am to 3 pm each day and 6 pm to 11 pm on Monday to Saturday (10.30 pm on Sunday). Fido is asked to stay and admire the view outside, but children are welcome and there is a play area.

✆ 01926 612428.

How to get there: The pub is 4 miles south-east of Leamington Spa along the A425, Daventry road.
Parking: There is a large car park behind the pub.
Length of the walk: 3 miles. Map: OS Landranger series 151 Stratford-upon-Avon and surrounding area (GR 379622).

THE WALK

1 From the car park, go to the main road and turn left. At the roundabout, cross to the lane signed to **Ufton Fields**. Within ½ mile, the lane bends sharp left.

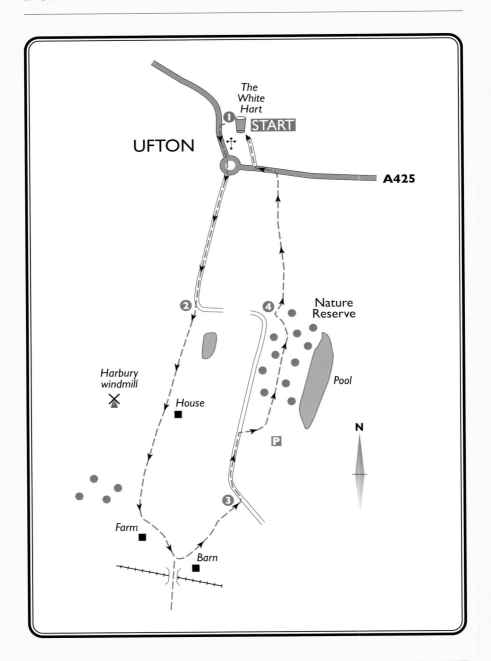

The White Hart

START

UFTON

A425

② Harbury windmill

House

Nature Reserve

Pool

③

P

N

Farm

Barn

④

2 Here, go through a kissing-gate to a meadow on the right. Follow the direction indicated, with a pool where wildfowl play away to the left. Walk to a gate in the opposite boundary and walk by a left-hand hedge. Maintain the direction, passing a white house. Further arrows show the way. Perched on a ridge ahead is the tower of **Harbury windmill**. Join a cart track and follow this to a farmstead. The track bears to the left of barns. Just before a railway bridge, leave the **Centenary Way** by taking a signed path to the left. After two more stiles, bear left to go over a stile. Continue across the field. In the next field walk by a right-hand hedge to a lane.

3 Turn left. Within ⅓ mile turn right to the car park of **Ufton Nature Reserve**. Go through a kissing-gate to the left. Follow near a right-hand pool. At a junction of ways go left through a kissing-gate to a meeting of paths. Take the track to the right. This is the **Centenary Way**. When the path divides, take the left-hand fork to pass through a kissing-gate. Beyond a seat, the path divides again. Take the left-hand fork to immediately go out of the reserve.

4 Follow the well-walked path to the **A425**. Turn left. Within 100 yards, take a lane on the right. This is **White Hart Lane** and will take you to the **White Hart** pub.

The Crown Inn

T<small>HE WALK CLIMBS THE</small> 500 <small>FT</small> N<small>APTON</small> H<small>ILL</small> (N<small>APTON MEANS</small> '<small>VILLAGE ON THE HILLTOP</small>') <small>WHERE THERE ARE TWO TOWERS.</small> <small>THE TOWER OF THE CHURCH OF</small> S<small>T</small> L<small>AWRENCE DATES FROM THE</small> 18<small>TH CENTURY AND A FIELD OR SO AWAY IS THE BEAUTIFULLY</small> <small>RESTORED WINDMILL DATING BACK TO</small> 1543. W<small>HETHER WE</small> <small>CHOOSE THE LONGER OR THE SHORTER ROUTE FOR THE RETURN,</small> <small>WE WALK ALONG THE TOWPATH OF THE</small> O<small>XFORD</small> C<small>ANAL</small>. T<small>HE</small> <small>WATERWAY WAS CONSTRUCTED IN THE</small> 18<small>TH CENTURY AND THE</small> <small>BARGES HAD A LONG TORTUOUS ROUTE, THE CANAL BEING BUILT AS</small> <small>A CONTOUR CANAL RATHER THAN A</small> '<small>CUT</small>' <small>ONE.</small>

I was attracted to the **CROWN INN** by its wonderful summer display of window boxes and hanging baskets and its charming location. The same family has been involved with the Crown since 1923. This is a typical village country inn, where locals gather to put the world to rights, take refreshments and get involved in those pub games – games which are rapidly disappearing in many pubs to give more space to the restaurant areas. The landlord is eager to tell customers that the Crown is haunted by its very own ghost. Food is traditional and just right for hungry walkers. Try the filled baps. There is always a good selection of real ales with several guest beers which are changed often. There are benches and tables on the front green for those warmer days and Meg was pleased that dogs are allowed inside on those not so summery days.

✆ 01926 815711.

How to get there: Napton-on-the-Hill is on the A425 Daventry to Leamington Spa road. The pub is on the little green in the centre of the village.

Parking: By the pub.

Length of the walk: 4 or 7 miles. Map: OS Landranger series 151 Stratford-upon-Avon and surrounding area (GR 465610).

THE WALK

1 From the pub turn right along the main street then drop downhill. At a T-junction turn left along **Dog Lane**. At the end of houses on the right take the signed bridleway along a track. Go over a brook then keep ahead. As the track swings left go ahead through a metal gate. The route is now beside hedges. Pass through another gate then a third. Turn left with a hedge on your left side. Go through a corner gate and at once go right to pass a pool. Go through a hunting gate over a brook. Walk at the side of the field and through a metal gate. Turn right.

2 In a large flat sheep pasture follow the side of the right-hand wire fence to pass a pool where cup and saucer lilies thrive to a

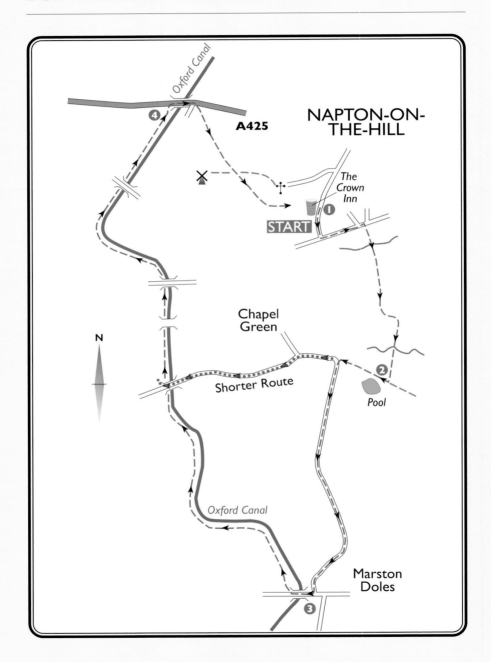

NAPTON-ON-
THE-HILL

A425

The
Crown
Inn

START

Oxford Canal

Chapel
Green

Shorter Route

Pool

N

Oxford Canal

Marston
Doles

gate onto a lane. Here you can choose either to return by way of **Chapel Green** or to continue on to **Marston Doles** to enjoy a longer stretch of canalside walking on the return journey.

For the shorter walk turn right on the lane to **Chapel Green**. Follow the lane back to the **Crown Inn** on the green at **Napton**.

NEAR NAPTON WINDMILL

3 *For the longer walk* turn left to reach the canal at **Marston Doles**. Gain the towing path and continue with the water on your right side to the bridge at the A425.

4 Cross the main road and turn left to go over the canal. Within 200 yards go over a stile by a road to an industrial estate. The path is signed. Climb the ridge and furrow pasture to a gate to a meadow. Maintain the heading to another gate. Through this bear 45° left to a gate in the opposite boundary. In a sheep pasture, walk parallel to the right-hand wire fence to a gate onto a lane. We turn left (but you might like to go a few steps right to have a closer look at the lovely windmill). The lane divides – keep right. (The rather fine **church of St Lawrence** is along the left fork.) Our lane drops down to the green and the **Crown Inn**.

The Shakespeare

THIS ROUTE IS THROUGH THE COUNTRY TOWN, THEN OVER MEADOWS AND ARABLE FIELDS. WE PASS THE SITE OF THE LONG-DEMOLISHED MANSION OF THE PEYTOS TO THEIR LARGE CHURCH AT CHESTERTON. HERE THERE ARE THE MAGNIFICENT TOMBS OF THE FAMILY AND A FINE GATEWAY TO A DESIGN BY INIGO JONES.

The building that houses the **SHAKESPEARE** is around 500 years old. It has been an inn for just over a century. The ambience is cosy, with a lot of old woodwork and nooks where the world's problems can be forgotten. Log fires blaze in the wintertime and the garden room is a pleasant dining area. This is a typical rural pub with plenty of activities for the locals. There are darts and pool, football and tug o' war teams. At the summer fête the pub enters a decorated float.

The pub has built up a good reputation for its friendly atmosphere and the culinary delights – all home-made – including the magnificent steak and kidney pie. The children's menu has all the favourites and they especially love the chicken drumsticks, followed by the fruity Shakespeare cocktail. The choice of real ales includes Flowers IPA, Timothy Taylor Landlord and guests. There are pleasant gardens at the back to amuse the children and dogs are allowed if well behaved. The opening hours are 12 noon to 3 pm Tuesday to Thursday; evenings 6.30 pm to late. Closed Monday. Open all day Friday, Saturday and Sunday.
℘ 01926 612357.

How to get there: Harbury is 7 miles south-east of Leamington Spa and can be reached from the A425 along the B4452. The Shakespeare is in Mill Street in the centre of the town.
Parking: There is a car park behind the pub.
Length of the walk: 5½ miles. Map: OS Landranger series 151 Stratford-upon-Avon and surrounding area (GR 372600).

THE WALK

1. From the car park, turn right in **Mill Street** then at once right again along **Chapel Street**. At the T-junction continue right, along **Park Lane**. Follow the road almost out of the town to climb a stile on the left. Walk through several fields, with stiles showing the way, with a hidden willow-fringed brook on the left. Go over a bridge and stile onto a road. Go right a step or so, then take a signed bridleway on the left. Just ½ mile along the road is the magnificent Chesterton Mill. The path hugs the left-hand hedge then goes around the corner to a cottage.

   Follow the path around the cottage to a field. It was to the left that the great Peyton house was situated until its destruction in 1902. Now only a garden wall remains to mark the spot.

PUB WALKS IN WARWICKSHIRE

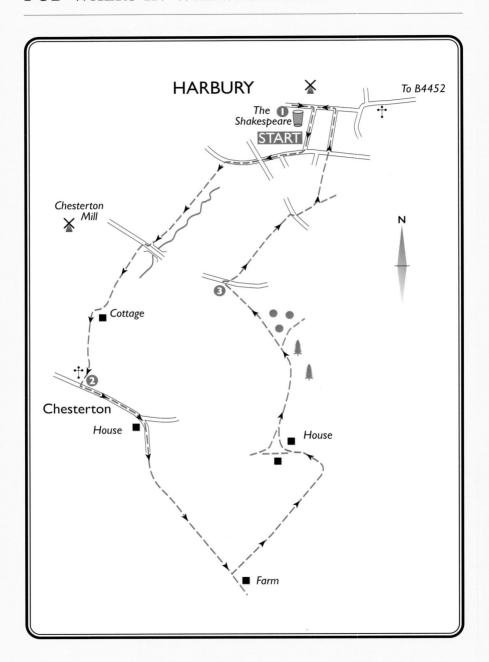

Bearing left, drop down the field to a bridge over the brook. Aiming to the left of the church and **Peyto gateway** (restored in 1990), go through a lych gate to the churchyard. Follow the arrowed way to a lane.

2 Turn left, with pools for wildfowl on the right side. Walk along the estate road over a cattle grid. At a junction by a house, take the right-hand fork to a farm. Go to the left, still along the farm roads. At a Y-junction, walk left and stay on the 'road' to pass woods. A step or two further (by a private drive),

NEAR NAPTON WINDMILL

go through a white metal gate to a field on the left. At once, turn right to follow the edge of fields to a road.

3 Turn right for 150 yards. Look for a signed path over a stile on the left. The path goes direct to a road. A step or two to the right, take another path across an arable field. A few yards past a solitary oak, turn left over a stile. Walk to a road. Cross to **Ivy Lane** opposite. This leads to the **Bull Ring** and a junction. Turn left along **High Street** to the **Shakespeare**.

The Kings Head

YOU START THIS WALK BY STROLLING THROUGH THE PRETTY VILLAGE, WHICH WAS ONCE IMPORTANT ENOUGH TO HAVE A NORMAN CASTLE AND A REGULAR MARKET. THE ROUTE THEN CLIMBS ABOVE THE VALE, UP THE WOODED RIDGE CALLED ROUGH HILLS. OVER ARABLE LANDS, WE REACH THE HAMLET OF NEWNHAM. THE RETURN IS ALONG BRIDLEWAYS AND FOOTPATHS, WITH THE TOWER OF ASTON CANTLOW CHURCH ACTING AS A GUIDING BEACON.

———◦●◦———

The **KINGS HEAD** is part of our literary history, for it is said that here the parents of William Shakespeare held their wedding breakfast after the ceremony in the nearby church of St John the Baptist. The interior is full of old beams, oaken furniture and settles and gleaming brass. We find a huge inglenook and hidden corners, and, with stone-flagged floors, walkers feel welcome. Outside there is a massive spreading chestnut tree (which offers youngsters prize-sized conkers in autumn) and the 14th-century building is swathed in hanging Virginia creeper.

The food menu offers good-value, traditional pub fare. There are always items for vegetarians, and children have their own menu. In the garden there are plenty of benches and tables. There is no firm rule on well-behaved dogs – ask the landlord is the answer. The real ales sold are Brew XI, Purity Gold and Abbot. There is Magners cider on draught. The opening hours are 12 noon to 2.30 pm and 6.30 pm to 11 pm (Monday to Saturday). Sunday 12.30 pm to 3 pm and 6 pm to 11 pm (no food Sunday evening).
⌀ 01789 488242.

How to get there: Aston Cantlow is signposted from the B4089 Wootton Wawen to Alcester road, south of Henley-in-Arden. The pub is in the centre of the village.
Parking: There is a car park behind the pub.
Length of the walk: 5½ miles. Map: OS Landranger series 151 Stratford-upon-Avon and surrounding area (GR 139599).

THE WALK

1 From the car park, turn left a yard or two along **Church Lane** to the main street. Turn left, with the pub now on the left. Walk to the far end of the village. When the houses end on the right, turn right along a track signed as an unclassified country road. Walk directly away from the road. The wide track goes through a gateway (no gate). Turn left along the left-hand hedge, then go 90° to the right in a corner. Continue alongside a left-hand hedge. Through a corner gateway (again no gate), follow the cart track through bushes to the top of the ridge, from where there is an excellent view.

Proceed by a left-hand hedge and keep a constant heading

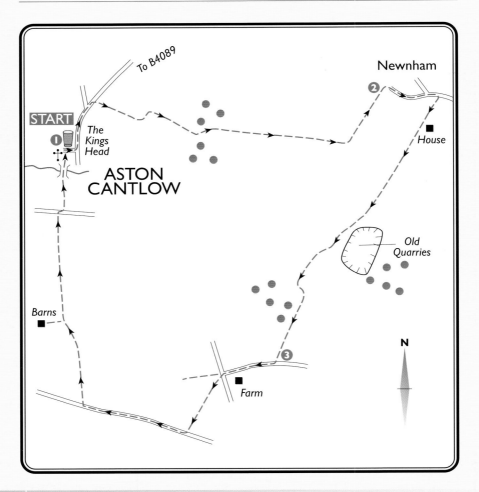

along a clear track. The route goes over open arable fields. On the far side, the way of tractors turns sharp left. Follow the farm track around bends to **Newnham**.

2 Keep ahead past the little green. Within a few steps, turn right, down a farm drive. Continue past a house and along a bridleway. The direction is fairly constant around the edge of fields. Soon there is a hidden quarry on the left and a reassuring

MEG SHOWS THE WAY TO ASTON CANTLOW

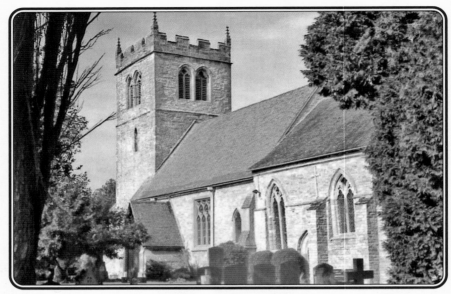

ASTON CANTLOW CHURCH

waymark arrow. Climb a step stile by woods to descend over arable lands to a lane.

3. Turn right. At a junction cross to the opposite path. Within 75 yards take the left-hand direction, to walk alongside a right-hand hedge to a stile into a lane. Turn right. Within ½ mile, take a signed path over a stile on the right. Walk beside a left-hand hedge to join a cart track.

Keep ahead to a lane. Turn right for a couple of steps, then go over a stile to a meadow. Walk the length of it to a stile and bridge under a large willow tree. Keep ahead along a path through the churchyard. Through the lych gate is **Church Lane** and the **Kings Head** is a few steps to the right.

The Black Horse

This walk is over some gently attractive countryside. This is intensively farmed land – mixed and arable. The walk goes by a most delightfully sited cricket ground, bordered by a brook at Ashorne, where you may be tempted to linger awhile. On the return route we pass Newbold Pacey church, which was designed by J.L. Pearson, the architect of Truro cathedral.

—•●•—

The **BLACK HORSE**, once called the Sea Horse, is tucked between houses in the main village street, rubbing eaves with a thatched cottage. It is thus a humble village inn with few pretensions, run by a landlord who knows what locals and travellers (including ramblers) want.

> **How to get there:** Moreton Morrell is along a lane, 1 mile off the Fosse Way and 7 miles south of Warwick. The pub is in the centre of the village.
> **Parking:** The pub has no car park but you can leave your car in the quiet street outside.
> **Length of the walk:** 4 miles. Map: OS Landranger series 151 Stratford-upon-Avon and surrounding area (GR 311559).

There is a small and cosy bar, the fount of current news both parochial and national, with wooden settles and chairs, and a games room where pool and dominoes are played at the rear. The choice of real ales in this freehouse is between Hook Norton Bitter and a guest beer, which is regularly changed, although the Shepherd Neame from far away Faversham is a popular choice. The cider is Strongbow (on draught). Tea and coffee are also available (in mugs, of course). The landlord is of the opinion that pubs are pubs rather than restaurants, but I must say that the simple fare offered is ideal for ramblers. The filled baps are the finest I have found on my walks, and hot pies sound ideal after a wintertime ramble. The pub, because space is so limited, is not suitable for children, and dogs cannot be admitted (no doubt the house collie cross would also object). The opening hours are 12 noon to 3 pm and 7 pm to 11 pm every day.

✆ 01926 651231.

THE WALK

1 Walk northwards along the main street and turn right, along **Brook Lane.** Within 200 yards, take a signed path on the left. In the pasture, walk alongside the left-hand border, with a barn on the right, to a far corner stile. Follow the well-waymarked route to a lane. Turn right. Within a few steps, by a junction, a path

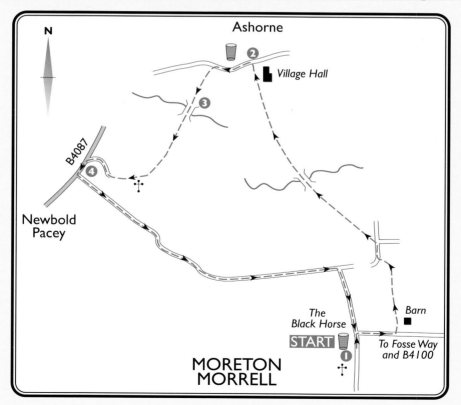

is signed over a stile on the left. Take the arrowed direction. The path is through sheep pastures, then crosses a brook over a footbridge. Beyond, walk through fields, taking the yellow arrowed headings. The path leads to a gate by the village hall at **Ashorne**.

2 Turn left to walk along the main street of the hamlet, passing an inn. About 100 yards beyond and at the end of the hamlet, a path starts on the left. It is signed through a little metal gate, then crosses the picturesque cricket field. Aim to the left of the pavilion.

3 Cross the brook. The well-used track keeps at the border of a field. Ignore a stile on the right and continue at the side of the field. The path leads to the church at **Newbold Pacey**. Keep the church on the left and proceed to the drive. Walk along the drive, passing cottages and a little green on the way to the B4087.

4 Turn left, then immediately left again along a lane signed to **Moreton Morrell**. Glance right and you may catch a glimpse of **Moreton Hall**. It was built in 1906 for an American (Mr Garland), and included one of the rare real tennis courts. The building now houses a large agricultural college. At the junction, turn right to the village and the **Black Horse**.

The Three Horseshoes

A NARROW LANE LEADS TO A CHURCH (SADLY OFTEN LOCKED) WHERE THERE ARE UNIQUE TREASURES – HUGE CANOPIED BRASSES OF THOMAS DE CREWE AND HIS WIFE. THE WALK CONTINUES ALONG THE TRACK WHICH WAS THE ROMANS' RYKNILD STREET, THEN OVER HILLS TO LITTLE EXHALL VILLAGE.

❖

The **THREE HORSESHOES** suggests the blacksmith's craft and – sure enough – we find the old forge (with the ancient tools of the trade) incorporated into this very attractive, restored building, which was once part of the Throckmorton Estate. They still talk of Jack Robbins hereabouts. He was the blacksmith for a long time and his wife Molly ran the adjoining pub for over 50 years, until 1983. This is an inn which preserves the best of the old with the best of the new and also gives a positive and unstinted welcome to walkers. This is one of the Task Inns' hostelries and the landlord does not mind a bit of footpath mud on the stone-flagged floors and even has a special stile to lead walkers towards the hostelry. All the food is fresh and home-cooked – frozen food is eschewed!

The huge menu is interesting and enterprising but the favourite items are still the home-made pies, the choice of steak and kidney, chicken and vegetable, and ham and mushroom, all delicious, making the selection difficult. There are plenty of goodies, too, for the vegetarian taste, and a children's menu. The youngsters' meals can be taken in the family room or in the family garden. The beers available in this house include Bombardier, IPA, Wye Valley Ales and several guests. Dogs must stay outside to admire the garden (sorry Fido and Meg), but it is truly delightful, with a tumbling stream flowing through the grounds. Open 12 noon to late every day.

✆ 01789 490400.

How to get there: Wixford is 2 miles north of Bidford on Avon and is on the B4085, which runs between the A439 and the A435. The pub lies on the south side of the village.

Parking: There is a car park at the front and side of the pub.

Length of the walk: 3½ miles. Map: OS Landranger series 150 Worcester and the Malverns (GR 092545).

THE WALK

1 Leave the car park at the exit furthest from the pub. Cross to the lane signed as a 'no through road'. At the end is Wixford's humble church. Keep ahead along the banked track which is **Ryknild Street**. After a little over ½ mile (where there is a small brick barn on the left), a signed junction of ways is reached. In

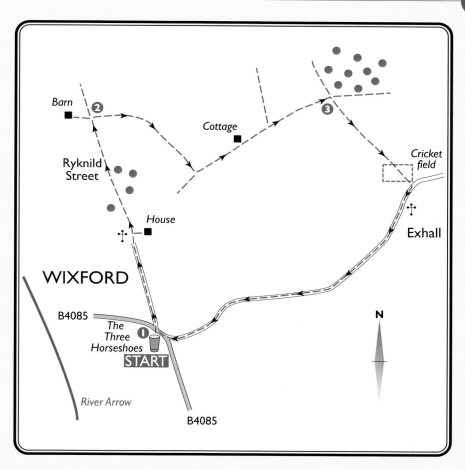

the field to the left is the mound on which the Norman Ralph de Botoler's castle was perched.

2 Turn right, along a cart track which is signed as a footpath. At a junction of wide tracks, turn left. We have now gained some height so there is a good view over the valley, with the 17th-century **Ragley Hall** prominent. Pass a cottage on the left. Shortly after, the main farm 'road' bends sharp left. Maintain the former direction ahead along a signed footpath.

THE RIVER ARROW AT WIXFORD

3 Immediately before a wood, turn right. The footpath, which may be unsigned, goes at the side of an arable field alongside a left-hand hedge. Over the ridge is a splendid view across the Avon vale to the Cotswolds. In a corner climb a stile, then turn right a step or two to go over another. Regain the old direction to drop down the hill to a stile to a cricket field.

Continue to a short vehicle track to a lane at **Exhall**, once named 'Dodging Exhall' because of its inaccessibility. Turn right to pass the 12th-century church. Follow the twisting lane to a junction. Bear right to the B4085 and the **Three Horseshoes**.

The Castle Inn

This walk starts along a high wooded ridge with many clearances for lovely views across the valley, where the great battle of Edge Hill took place on Sunday 23rd October 1642. The actual site, however, is on Ministry of Defence land and not open to the public. The return is across farmland where the paths are not so clearly defined.

———— ◆ ————

The **CASTLE INN** is a pub steeped in history. The battle of Edge Hill was the opening skirmish of the Civil War in 1642 and it is on the site of the Castle Inn that King Charles raised the Royalist standard before his troops descended into the vale where the Parliamentarians were assembled under Lord Essex. The inn itself is a sham castle, built by Sanderson Miller a hundred years after the battle, and modelled on Guy's Tower at Warwick Castle. One bar is a reminder of the war, with maps of the battle strategem, a fine mural of the fighting and numerous pistols, swords and breastplates of the period. The second bar depicts more peaceful and rustic pursuits, with the walls adorned with agricultural implements. There is one interesting later feature – a print of an aircraft. The Pioneer was one of the first experimental jet aircraft and it was at Edge Hill airfield (long closed by the Royal Air Force) that much of the test flying was undertaken in 1942.

The stone pub, first licensed in 1822, may have a rugged, weather-worn exterior but inside there has been an extensive refurbishing operation by the Hook Norton Brewery. There is a warm cosy look about the beamed bars, the carpets are a homely red and an open fire blazes in the wintertime. Great pride is taken in the food. The menu concentrates on simple, wholesome meals and folk travel many miles along the lanes to sample the home-cooked gammon and pies. The mixed grill is also recommended, the 'mix' being of such generous proportions that the plates are extra large – sounds tempting doesn't it after walking the last mile up the steep hill? Children are especially catered for and they invariably plump for the beans on toast with sausage. There is always a vegetarian dish available. The beers on offer are the real ale Hook Horton Bitter and John Smith's, and there is also always a guest beer from the Independent Family Brewers of Britain. In addition there are country wines, such as dandelion and cowslip and, for something stronger, an extensive range of malt whiskies. Opening hours are flexible but are based on 11.30 am to 2.30 pm and 6.30 pm to 11 pm.

Choose the right day for your walk and sit in the lovely hilltop garden for your refreshment, where the views are truly magnificent – and your cares will be forgotten. My well-behaved collie Meg was made most welcome and concurs with my observations.

✆ 01295 670255.

> **How to get there:** Edge Hill lies between the A422 Banbury–Stratford road and the B4086. It is signposted from Sun Rising Hill, the steep ridge 6 miles north-west of Banbury.
> **Parking:** The car park is opposite the pub.
> **Length of the walk:** 4 miles. Map: OS Landranger series 151 Stratford-upon-Avon and surrounding area (GR 373474).

THE WALK

1 From the car park, cross the road to a signed path. Within a step or two, keep ahead now on the **Centenary Way**. The path is along a raised concrete path. When the way divides, take the left-hand track. The path twists a well-walked way to a tarmac vehicle track. Turn left for 100 yards, then turn right along a signed path bordering a farm.

2 The path keeps near the edge of woodlands to the A422 at **Sun Rising** (there was once an inn of this name here). Drop down the hill for ⅓ mile. Take care as this is a busy road. There is a signed path on the right. A few yards further, take another path (directly opposite a road on the left) through a wide hedge gap.

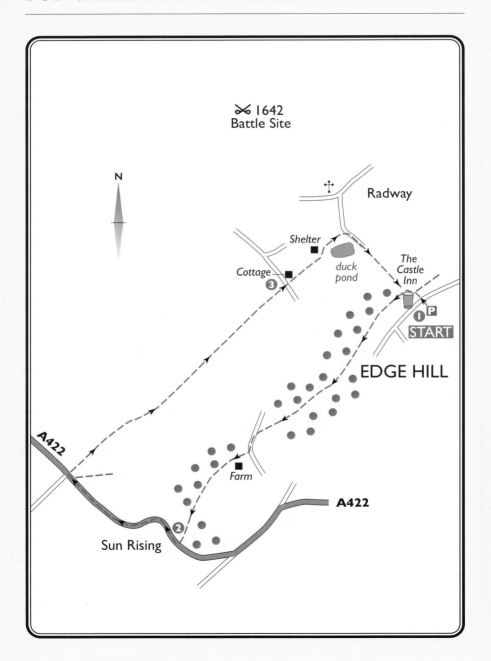

⚔ 1642
Battle Site

N

Radway

Shelter

Cottage

❸

duck
pond

The
Castle
Inn

❶ P
START

EDGE HILL

A422

Farm

A422

❷

Sun Rising

THE VIEW FROM THE CASTLE INN

Walk alongside a right-hand hedge. When this ends, maintain the heading over an open field. Aim to the right of a distant spire. Go over a ditch and through a hedge gap on the far side. Bear right to the far right-hand corner of a field. Under a willow tree, climb a fence stile. Continue ahead for a few yards to go through an old metal railing gate. Walk alongside a left-hand hedge to gates to a lane.

3 Cross directly over to go through a gate to the right of a cottage. Keep ahead through a kissing-gate to sheep pastures. Maintain the heading to pass to the right of a brick animal shelter. Climb a corner stile, then keep ahead to another.

The path is now bordered by gravestones. This was the site of the old Radway church, where the bells are said to have rung when the king's troops passed by. A new church was built on another site in 1866.

On a lane by a duck pond, turn right. At the end of the lane, go through a kissing-gate. Now aiming for the pub tower, climb through pastures to a stile by woods. Join the outward path to return to the **Castle Inn**.

AUTUMN ON EDGE HILL

The Red Lion

I THINK THE COUNTRYSIDE AROUND ILMINGTON IS THE BEST IN
WARWICKSHIRE FOR RAMBLING. THIS WALK CLIMBS STEEPLY
THROUGH SHEEPLANDS TO ILMINGTON DOWNS. ON THE WAY WE
PASS A POOL CONSTRUCTED SOME YEARS AGO. THERE IS MUCH
EVIDENCE OF BADGERS IN THIS ATTRACTIVE AREA.

The **RED LION** was, for most of its 200-year history, a basic
country inn, supplying the simple but wholesome wants of
agricultural workers. Indeed the Court Baron met here to discuss
who would farm where, prior to the Enclosure Acts. Although very
few villagers are now employed on the six farms in the vicinity, this
Hook Norton Brewery pub still has a rustic appearance, with small
bars and stone flags on the floor. The old blacksmith's shop next
door is now the inn's garage. There are prints of village scenes of
days long past and on the bar wall is a feature of the traditional

Ilmington morris dancers, who are to be seen and heard in the area in the summer months. Do the walk on the right Sunday in April and you will see them dancing in the ten village gardens open for charity.

The Red Lion is lovingly cared for, with a homely feel, masses of gleaming brass, open fires in winter, flowers from the lovely garden and tumbling blooms in baskets and window boxes in summer, and so on. You can join in traditional pub games here, too. The menu includes the usual pub fare and the gammon and eggs is popular after the hike up the hills – the modest prices are also very popular. The real ales are Old Hooky and Hooky Best Bitter. Well-behaved children (and dogs) are welcome. The hours of opening are flexible but the pub is open all day in summer.

✆ 01608 682366.

How to get there: Ilmington is 8 miles from Stratford. The turning from the A3400 is signposted 4 miles to the south. The Red Lion is on the right in the village.
Parking: Very limited parking is available in front of the pub. Otherwise you can park on the road.
Length of the walk: 3 miles. Map: OS Landranger series 151 Stratford-upon-Avon and surrounding area (GR 212435).

THE WALK

1) From the **Red Lion**, take the lane signed to **Shipston**. We cross a hidden brook, which once supplied the water for sheep dipping, then bear right along a narrow road (signed **Compton Scorpion**). After 1½ miles and opposite **Southfields Farm**, a footpath is signed on the right, through a gate. Follow the way of tractors then follow signs to a pool.

2) Swing left (with the pool now on the right) and cross the little rivulet at the far end. The faint path now leads to a corner gate to sheep pastures. Climb the hill, keeping near the left-hand

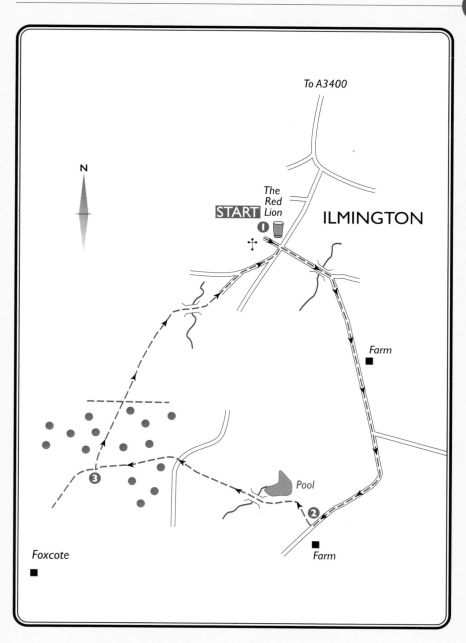

border. At the top of the ridge climb a stile on a lane and cross to the drive opposite – this is also signed as a footpath. Within ⅓ mile, take a path to the right. (The large mansion in the vale is **Foxcote**, built in the Palladian style in the early 18th century.)

(3) Climb the edge of a usually arable field, keeping by a right-hand border. At the summit cross a wide track. Walk alongside a right-hand hedge. Walk through meadowland, gradually dropping down the hill. Ignore a path going to the right, and continue to a footbridge to cross a brook. Over the water, at once turn left to a corner gate – a bit boggy here. Follow the well-used and waymarked path ahead to meet a lane to **Ilmington** and a well-deserved drink at the **Red Lion**.

ILMINGTON

The Black Horse

SHIPSTON WAS A PLACE WHICH BECAME PROSPEROUS FROM THE SHEEP AND WOOL INDUSTRY. THE CHURCH TOWER HAS LOOKED OVER THE TOWN FOR 500 YEARS. THE WALK IS ALONG THE VALLEY OF THE RIVER STOUR AND WE VISIT ANOTHER OLD CHURCH – BARCHESTON HAS A PISA-LIKE LEANING TOWER. THE VILLAGE WITNESSED THE BIRTH OF TAPESTRY WEAVING IN ENGLAND WHEN WILLIAM SHELDON SET UP HIS LOOMS IN THE 16TH CENTURY.

The **BLACK HORSE** is a lovely, thatched-roofed inn that is of great antiquity (built in the 1700s) and surrounded by fairly newly-constructed buildings. The road outside until half a century or so ago would have led to the railway station at the end of the now defunct branch line.

Today the pub is a popular local. Inside there are low ceilings (so guard your head!) and heavy timbers – and a very warm welcome from a traditional English pub awaits you. There is talk of a friendly ghost – a lady – who moves objects around. We find here a very comprehensive menu with a 'specials board' and children can choose their favourites. The beers are Flowers IPA and Adnams. The pub is open Monday to Friday 11 am to 3 pm and from 5.30 pm to 12 midnight. On Saturday the Black Horse is open all day and Sunday hours are from 12 noon to 3 pm and 7 pm to 12 midnight.

⌀ 01608 662732.

How to get there: The Black Horse is reached along the A3400 and then along Watery Lane.
Parking: There is a car park in front of the inn.
Length of the walk: 3½ miles. Map: OS Landranger series 151 Stratford-upon-Avon and surrounding area (GR 258407).

THE WALK

1 Walk along **Watery Lane** by the inn. At the main road turn right to pass the church. Bear left along the B4035 to cross the bridge over the **river Stour**. Within 200 yards, go through a kissing-gate to a pasture on the right. Take the arrowed direction, keeping by right-hand borders, with the river away to the right. Further stiles and gates show the way through the fields. When in a sheep pasture, with a church tower directly on the left, bear left to the far left corner. Here there is a stile onto a vehicle track.

2 Within a step or two the track leads to a lane. Follow this left. We go by the church whose tower leans about 1 ft in 50 ft, but we are assured it has not moved for 200 years. At a junction take the right-hand fork. **Brailes Hill** – one of the highest hills in the county – is on the far horizon.

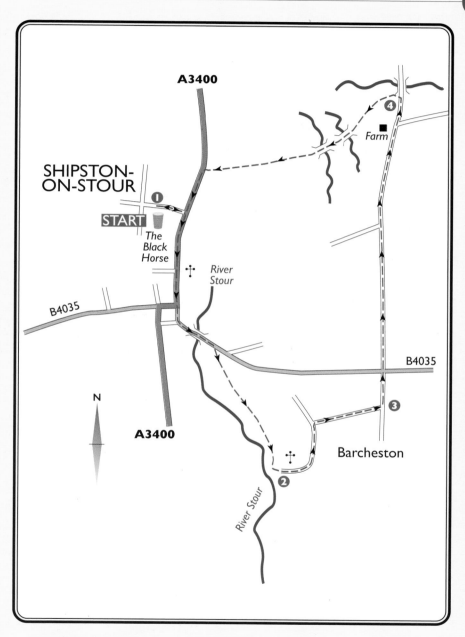

A3400

SHIPSTON-
ON-STOUR

1

START The Black Horse

Farm

4

B4035

River Stour

B4035

N

A3400

3

2

River Stour

Barcheston

RIVER STOUR AT SHIPSTON-ON-STOUR

3 At a T-junction, turn left, then cross the B4035. Stay on the lane for about another mile, passing two junctions. Just before a railed bridge, the next path starts on the left. The gate is back from the lane.

4 In the meadow, continue to the far left corner to cross a footbridge. This is over waters which once powered **Fell Mill**. Take the indicated direction to go over the main channel of the river, where fine cup and saucer lilies bloom in summer. In a large pasture, keep by the right-hand border to a vehicle track to the A3400. Turn left to **Watery Lane** and the **Black Horse**.

The George Hotel

IN MEDIEVAL TIMES BRAILES WAS A THRIVING AND VERY PROSPEROUS WOOL TOWN – THE THIRD LARGEST IN THE COUNTY. THE MAGNIFICENT CHURCH IS EVIDENCE OF THIS WEALTH AND IS CALLED THE CATHEDRAL OF THE FELDON (THE FERTILE LAND IN THE SOUTH OF THE COUNTY). THERE ARE TWO HILLS OVERLOOKING THE AREA – ONE WAS TOPPED BY A MOTTE AND BAILEY CASTLE AND THE OTHER IS BRAILES HILL, WHICH IS THE SECOND-HIGHEST POINT IN THE COUNTY.

It is no coincidence that the church opposite the **GEORGE HOTEL** is dedicated to St George. In 1350 the masons building the church were housed in the pub building. Ale was dispensed on the site before this, because a market had been granted to Brailes in 1248, and the George claims to be one of the earliest ale houses in Warwickshire. During the age of the Royal Mail coaches, it was a celebrated coaching inn where there was extensive stabling. It may be ancient but it is undoubtedly also one of the nicest rural hotels with the comforts of today. It has nine en suite bedrooms and, in the gleaming stone-flagged restaurant and two bars of this Hook Norton house, there is a cosy ambience with huge inglenook fireplaces. The front of the hotel is bedecked with flowers in summertime and the rear gardens, where there are plenty of benches and tables, are a delight and have a winding level path with disabled folk in mind.

Four Hook Norton real ales are served, together with a brand of guest beers which is changed periodically. The food is all prepared on the premises and local produce is used for the English fare served, where possible. The favourite is honey roast duck. The pub is open all day, every day (12 noon to 11 pm). Dogs are welcome on leads. Children are welcome without leads and can have small portions from the menu. Note – walkers are especially welcome here.

✆ 01608 685223.

How to get there: Lower Brailes lies east of Upper Brailes, on the B4035 Shipston to Banbury road. The George Hotel is in the centre of the village, almost opposite the church.
Parking: The car park is at the side of the pub.
Length of the walk: 3½ miles. Map: OS Landranger series 151 Stratford-upon-Avon and surrounding area (GR 313392).

THE WALK

1 Alongside the pub, near the archway through which coaches trundled, take the unsigned footpath. Soon go over a stile and continue to the end of the wall, where there is a junction of pathways. Take the way to the left to cross a brook and climb a stile to a meadow. Turn right at once, with the brook now on

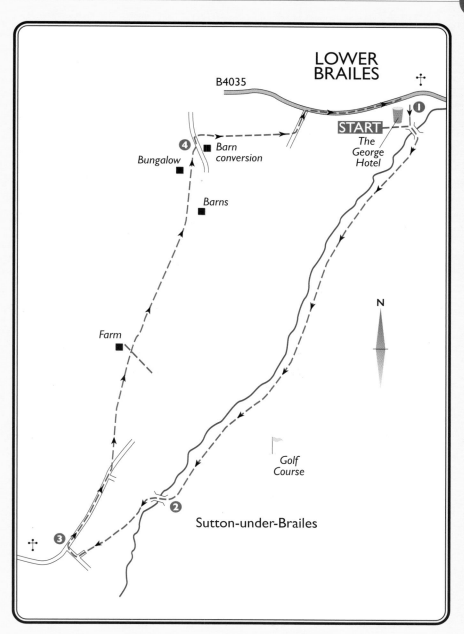

your right-hand side. The next field is often sown. Keep ahead to a rather hidden fence stile in the far right-hand corner. Join a farm drive and, as this sweeps left to the farm, maintain the old direction to pass through a metal gate. At the bottom of a field go over a stile to a golf course. Keep the former direction, with the brook still to the right, to a stile out of the golf course onto a cart track. Turn right, then at once left over a stile into a rough pasture.

2 Bear right to cross the brook over a railing bridge. Gradually leave the brook, with a farmstead away to the right, to reach a rough metal fence, then go over a ditch and a step stile into a pasture. Follow the arrowed direction to join a cul-de-sac lane by a cottage. Follow the lane a few steps to a T-junction. Turn right to the village of **Sutton-under-Brailes**.

BRAILES CHURCH

3 At a T-junction, the 13th-century church is to the left but we turn right. Within ¼ mile, the next path is over a stile on the left. Take a direction half-right to cross an open field, aiming for a point to the right of a distant farmhouse. Climb a stile under a tree and maintain the direction to cross the farm drive.

Go over a little pasture to pass through a large arable field. Still the direction is constant, passing just to the right of two isolated trees to a distant stile. Cross a sheep pasture to a step stile, then another field, making for just to the left of distant barns. Maintain this heading over fields towards a point to the right of a far bungalow. Go through a bridle gate to a lane.

4 Turn left for a few steps. At the far side of a barn conversion on the right, climb a stile. Take the signed direction. Stiles show the route (now aiming towards the church tower). Pick up the line of a left-hand hedge, then walk at the side of gardens to a road. Turn left to the B4035. **Lower Brailes** and the **George Hotel** are to the right.

The Cherington Arms

CHERINGTON HAS NOTHING TO DO WITH CHERRIES – IN SPITE OF THE PUB SIGN OF A BUXOM LADY WITH AN ARMFUL OF FRUIT. IT MEANS 'A VILLAGE OF THE CHURCH'. THIS 13TH-CENTURY BUILDING IS ACROSS A MEADOW. THE WALK FOLLOWS THE VALLEY OF THE STOUR TO SUTTON-UNDER-BRAILES, BRAILES BEING THE HILL WHICH WE THEN CLIMB TO GIVE US THAT THIRST!

———— ◆◆ ————

The **CHERINGTON ARMS** looks very ancient – as indeed the building truly is – but it has only been the hostelry of the pretty little village since the last Great War. Before that it was a general store. There is a friendly, welcoming atmosphere at this Hook Norton tenancy. The bar has a utilitarian tiled floor to withstand walking boots and there are log fires in the inglenook fireplace in the winter months. The garden backing onto the river Stour is a peaceful haven on warmer days. It is big enough for youngsters to chase and play.

The reputation of the meals at the Cherington Arms is widespread. There is a bar menu, and all the meals are home-made. The vegetarians have a wide choice on the menu. Were I not to like my meat, I would probably be tempted by one of the options. The restaurant offers an even larger selection and, like the bar and lounge, the dining room is cosy and snug. A Sunday roast is also available every week. The opening hours are 12 noon to 2.30 pm and 6.30 pm to 11 pm (Monday to Saturday). Note – no food on Monday evenings. Sunday hours are 12 noon to 3 pm and 7 pm to 10.30 pm.

☎ 01608 686233.

How to get there: Cherington is signed from the A3400 just 1½ miles south of Shipston-on-Stour. A little after 2 miles you will see signs to the Cherington Arms.
Parking: The car park is opposite the pub.
Length of the walk: 3 miles. Map: OS Landranger series 151 Stratford-upon-Avon and surrounding area (GR 292369).

THE WALK

1 From the car park, turn right along the lane. Within ¼ mile, the lane bends sharp right. Keep ahead along a footpath beside a left-hand wall to pass a former chapel (now a house). Climb a stile into a pasture.

Bear left to the **river Stour**. Away to the right are the hollows and banks where there was once a moated house. Follow the river to the right and cross the water over a railed bridge. In the field, make for the double step-stile in the fence to the right of barns.

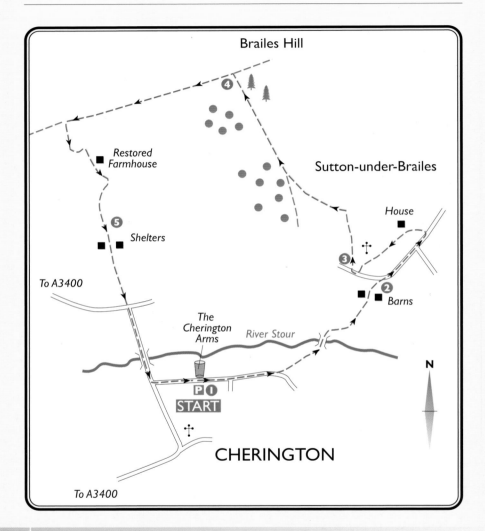

2 Bear left between the barns to the drive and continue to the green at **Sutton-under-Brailes**. Maintain the heading along the road to pass the war memorial. Soon after, turn left along a vehicle drive. Keep to the left of the house at the far end to walk along a fenced footpath to a churchyard. Follow the path past the church with its 14th-century tower, to a road.